HENNY YOUNGMAN'S

BAR BETS, BAR JOKES, BAR TRICKS

HENNY YOUNGMAN'S

BAR BETS, BAR JOKES, BAR TRICKS

by Henny Youngman

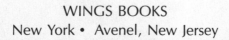

Illustrated by
Jerry Van Amerongen

WINGS BOOKS
New York • Avenel, New Jersey

This 1994 edition is published by Wings Books,
distributed by Random House Value Publishing, Inc.,
40 Engelhard Avenue, Avenel, New Jersey 07001,
by arrangement with the author.

Random House
New York • Toronto • London • Sydney • Auckland

Printed and bound in the United States of America

Library of Congress Cataloging-in-Publication Data

Youngman, Henny.
[Bar bets, bar jokes, bar tricks]
Henny Youngman's bar bets, bar jokes, bar tricks.
p.   cm.
Originally published: 1st ed. Secaucus, N.J. : Citadel Press, © 1974.
ISBN 0-517-10188-2
1. Conjuring.   2. Tricks.   3. Wit and humor.   4. Drinking customs.   I. Title.
GV1547.Y77   1994
793.8—dc20   94-3342
CIP

8 7 6 5 4 3 2 1

CONTENTS

Foreword   ix

HENNY YOUNGMAN'S

Bar Bets   1

Bar Jokes   47

Bar Tricks   93

NOW TAKE THIS BOOK . . . PLEASE!
. . . But First, PAY FOR IT!

You are sitting at a bar and you'd really love to strike up a conversation with that beautiful blonde! You are trying to get that stone-faced buyer to smile, at a business meeting! You are sitting at a dull party (at your own house, no less!) and you want everyone to get to know each other better! Or you are with the boys at the corner pub and you want to win a few free drinks (after all, payday isn't until Friday)!

O.K.! Step in a bit closer . . . you came to the right place!

That's why I am dedicating this collection of "Bar Bets, Bar Jokes, Bar Tricks" to you!

If you are a quiet, normal, level-headed human being, you usually avoid "baggy pants comedy" and a "Mr. Show Biz" attitude. But under all that calm exterior and even disposition lurks a bit of Hollywood and Broadway, all rolled into one. Everyone of us dreams of being a guest on the TV talk show or playing the "Big Room" at the Dunes or the T-Bird in Las Vegas (Me too, me too!).

Well, take my advice, go back to your job . . . stay in school . . . and don't come to New York. . . . Do you think I want *competition?* What I mean to say is, read the book, try out some of these puzzles and stunts when the occasion arises, and you just might become the center of attraction . . . you might pick up a few free drinks (of Coke, of course!), and that beautiful blonde may just give you a second glance (the rest is up to you . . . I'm a happily married man!).

RULES OF THE HOUSE

All of these "bar bits" have been gathered from collections dating back over one hundred years (sounds like Milton Berle's gagfile!). They have all been written in the form of wagers, bets or challenges. They appear to be difficult and some are, until the secret is revealed (which you don't; until you have won the game!). You use them as "ice-breakers," as simple games, or demonstrate them as "magic tricks." Your kids and your old-maid aunt will not be offended by them, as not one of these bets is off-color or in bad taste (some are a bit wacky, of course!). Keep the bet small, since some of the solutions to the stunts are a bit "far out," and some are just jokes made for laffs! Make sure your buddy is a good sport *before* you attempt the stunt, otherwise you risk the consequences of a "fist sandwich!"

And remember, all of the stunts are "just for fun" and should be presented in a light-hearted manner. Avoid a wise-guy, "the joke's on you" attitude which will defeat the entertainment value for your "audience." Who knows, they may start a fan club in your honor if they like you!

All of the bets use simple items like coins, matches and glasses; all found

FOREWORD

at home or at a lounge. Toothpicks or pretzel sticks may be substituted for matches. Sugar cubes, olives or "odds 'n' ends" may be used in place of coins (Remember . . . payday, Friday!). Make everything nice and easy for yourself by preparing your "props" before you plan to "go on"! Do not, I repeat, do *not* force these stunts on your friends! Wait until the right moment to perform, when they will fully appreciate your "artistry."

Then remember, go back to your job, stay in school and above all, stay out of show business. . . . I need every dollar I can get!

HENNY

HENNY YOUNGMAN'S

BAR
BETS

EGG CREAM

Bet that you can make an egg float on water. When all bets are covered, put the egg in a glass of water, and add loads of salt until the egg rises to the top.

EGG BALANCE

Ask everyone to try to balance an egg on end. When they fail, you can make the egg stand upright.

Secretly, before the bet is made, place some salt under the tablecloth. Stand the egg large end down over the salt, which helps to balance it.

STRONG THUMB

Have someone sit in a chair with his face looking up at the ceiling. Press your thumb hard on the center of his forehead above the bridge of the nose.

Challenge him to rise out of the chair without using his hands. It is quite difficult, if not impossible!

MONEY MAKER

Tell everyone to lay quarters heads down on a table. State that *you are willing to pay a dime for every quarter* whose date you can't name, sight unseen.

The more dates you fail to guess, the better you are. Because at the end, you pick up the quarters one by one and hand each owner a dime instead.

Remind them that you said, *"I will pay a dime for every quarter* whose date I couldn't name. I'm paying dimes for quarters."

SOMETHING FOR NOTHING

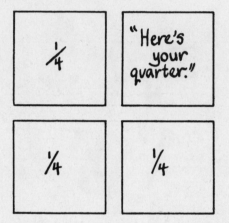

Bet someone that if he can tear a sheet of paper into four equal pieces, you will give him a quarter.

Naturally, anyone can come close to tearing the sheet into four equal pieces. So hand him a *quarter* (one of the four pieces of paper).

A quarter of the paper, right?

FIRE AND WATER

Bet that you can make water run up hill.

Pour water into a plate. Drop a burning piece of paper into a glass, and immediately invert the glass with the burning paper, and put it mouth down into the water-filled plate.

As the flame goes out, a vacuum forms and pulls the water up into the glass!

WHISKEY AND WATER

Fill one whiskey glass with whiskey and another with water. Challenge your barmates to transpose the water and whiskey without touching either liquid!

Here's how. Place a small square of cardboard (business card or playing card will do) on the glass of water. Holding the card to the glass to form a vacuum, turn the glass of water over and place it in this inverted position on top of the glass of whiskey with the card between.

Now, move the card slightly, so air is permitted to pass along one edge of the glass and over the edge of the card. *The two liquids will switch places!*

TAILS YOU LOSE

Place any coin, heads up, under a glass and cover the glass with a handkerchief. Bet that you can turn the coin tails-up without picking up the glass. Have someone place their hand on the handkerchief over the glass to prevent you from lifting it.

Now place your hand under the handkerchief and give the glass a slight turn. Remove the coin, and say, "It is done. Let's see if I win." As soon as they remove the handkerchief and lift the glass, immediately reach over and turn the coin tails-up, and say, "See, I win! I didn't lift the cup, you did!"

WET BET

Fill a glass of water or liquid right up to the brim.

   Place your bets as to how many coins can go into the water before the liquid spills over. All coin bets are dropped carefully, one at a time, into the glass. Many additional coins can be added before it spills over as the liquid swells up over the top of the glass rim.

HARD WATER

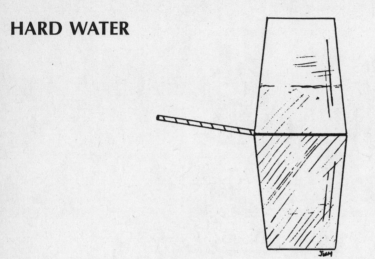

Fill a glass of water to the brim. Fill a second glass to the brim, and place a piece of stiff paper over the mouth of the second glass and invert it. The water does not fall out, even though the glass is upside-down.

Now place the inverted glass on top of the other, mouth to mouth. Pull the paper out slowly.

Now bet that you can drink all the water out of the top glass without lifting it off.

The secret is to place a drinking straw at the line where the rims meet and drink until all the water in the top glass is consumed.

THREE MATCHES

Borrow a quarter. Place it on the table and lay three matches around it, triangle fashion. Then bet a dime that they won't answer "three matches" to each of three questions.

First ask two ordinary questions to which the bettor will answer "three matches." Then ask "What will you take for your quarter?" If he says "three matches," give him the three matches and a dime (He wins the bet but loses fifteen cents).

If he won't say "three matches," he gets his quarter back, but he loses the dime bet.

CATCH A BUCK

Hold a dollar bill by one corner in your left hand. Let the rest of the bill dangle. Spread the thumb and forefinger of your right hand so that the fingers encircle the bill down at the bottom of the bill. Release bill from your left hand and show how easy it is to catch the bill between the thumb and forefinger. Catch the bill so that your thumb lands on Washington's picture.

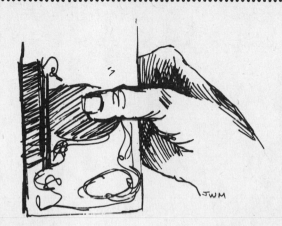

Now bet that they can't catch the bill while you drop it. Hold the corner of the bill, and tell the bettor to encircle the bill with his thumb and forefinger and try to catch the bill with the two fingers only. It's almost impossible to catch, if they don't cheat!

GRANDMA'S DOORMAT

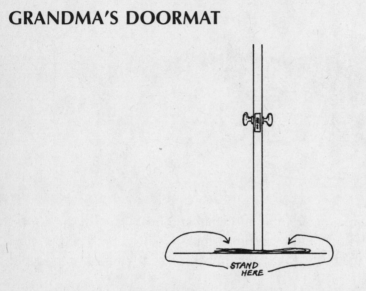

Bet someone that it's possible to place newspaper on the floor in such a way that two persons can stand on it together and yet not be able to touch each other.

The secret is to place the paper on the floor in a doorway and then close the door over it, with one person on each side of the door.

A QUICKIE!

Drink it!

Bet someone that he cannot pour a glass of liquid down his neck without getting wet. The solution . . . drink it!

THE PAPER ROPE

MOISTEN

Twist a paper napkin into a rope and invite anyone to break it with a steady pull. It is almost impossible!

That is, unless you first secretly moisten it near the center.

TIME OUT

Bet your friends that they cannot remember whether the number "6" on their watches is printed in Roman (VI) or Arabic (6) numerals.

The answer is that in many watches, the second hand occupies the 6 space! Naturally, it won't work with a watch with a "sweep second" hand.

INTO THE BOTTLE

Place a bottle on the floor inside a door and bet that you can crawl into it.

The demonstration looks silly, but get into the other room with the bottle opening facing toward you, and crawl *in to* it.

CIGARETTE BREAK

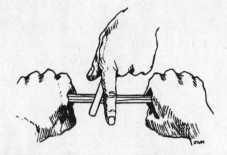

Have a friend hold the ends of a pencil between his two hands tightly, leaving about three inches of pencil showing. Hold a cigarette extended from your clenched fist, and bet that you can break the pencil with the cigarette.

With a quick "down-sweep," secretly extend your forefinger, breaking the pencil. Apparently the cigarette broke it!

WRITER'S CRAMP

Bet someone that you will tell him something he cannot write. Have him write, in numerals, the number eleven thousand, eleven hundred and eleven. The answer is 12,111.

Then ask him to write, "There are three 2's in the English language." There is no *correct* way to write the sentence or to spell (to, two, too), tuse or tuze!

COCKTAIL MIX

Bet your buddy that you can pour water on top of soda or liquor without mixing them—and then drink the drink and leave the water.

First, float a small piece of paper on the drink. Then carefully, with a spoon, put a film of water over this. You have poured water without mixing! To get the liquor or soda out, drink it from a straw.

STOOD UP

Bet that you can make someone come down from a chair by merely commanding "Get down!" (He has to come down sometime).

HOT FORK GAG

Place three forks on a table edge. Bet one of your guests that he cannot pick up the center one without using his hands.

Most people will use their teeth, so coat the underside of the center fork handle with hot mustard.

DIME DOWNFALL

Break a wooden match halfway through, but don't break it entirely. Form a V-shape and place the match on top of a small whiskey glass and put a dime on top of it.

Now bet that without touching the coin or the match, you can make the dime fall into the glass.

The secret is to drop some water on the split center of the match. The wood fibers will expand, and the dime will drop in!

COIN IN GLASS

INSIDE OF HAT

Balance a man's hat (or an open tin can) on its side, upon a glass. Then, carefully balance a coin on top of the hat (or can) directly above the glass. Give the hat a sharp blow and the hat will fly leaving the coin in the glass.

The secret is to give a very sharp quick blow *inside* the hat brim. Bet the bystanders to repeat your act! We bet they can't.

ANOTHER COIN DROP

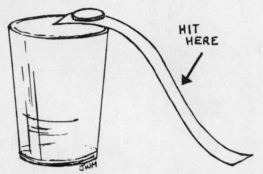

HIT HERE

Lay a heavy strip of paper on the edge of a glass. Balance a coin on the paper and edge of the glass.

When all bets are covered, strike a sharp downward blow at the midpoint and the coin will fall into the glass.

HEAVY!

Place an apple and an orange (or any two objects, for that matter) in front of your friend. Bet him that he cannot lift either of them alone.

You win—no matter which he lifts, you say, "You are not alone, I'm here!"

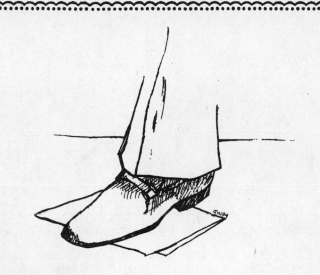

THE MINDREADER

Ask someone to write a message on a piece of paper, fold it, and stand on it. Then bet that you can tell him *what is on it*. The answer is "You are!"

A HOT ONE

Place a piece of paper on top of a glass. Now place a dime on top of the paper directly over the glass.

Bet that you can make the dime fall into the glass without touching the paper, glass or coin.

Ignite the paper with a match!

SUPERFINGERS

Have a woman place her hands firmly against her chest with the finger tips just touching. Bet someone that they cannot pull the hands apart. If the girl's wrists are grasped firmly, an attempt to pull the hands apart is close to impossible.

Do not stand sideways or attempt to jerk the hands, but exert a steady pull, at arm's length or with both arms bent to improve the leverage.

STRONG ARM

Bet someone that he cannot hold an ordinary book straight at arm's length, at shoulder height, for ten minutes. Impossible to do!

ANOTHER HOT ONE

Bet that you can set fire to a handkerchief without injuring it.

Dip part of a handkerchief in brandy, then set a light to it. The flame will spread all over it. When the alcohol is consumed, the moist part that remains will put the fire out.

THE MAGNETIZED GLASS

Bet your host that you can magnetize a glass. A glass with a hollow bottom is required. The bottom rim is slightly dampened before the stunt is performed. Press the palm down firmly upon the bottom and the slight vacuum formed will be strong enough to support the weight of the glass.

HEADS I WIN

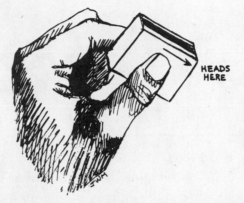

HEADS
HERE

Bet your buddy that you can tell which direction the heads of the matches in a box of safety matches are pointing without looking inside the box.

Shake the box and win every time since you can feel that the head ends are heavier than the tails by grasping the box very lightly in the center. The added weight of the head ends will lower one end of the box. Try it once or twice and you will even *hear* the difference!

P.S.: Use a full box.

TOSSING FOR DRINKS

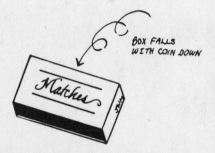 

BOX FALLS
WITH COIN DOWN

COIN
BETWEEN
DRAWER
AND
COVER

A box of safety matches thrown into the air will land on the table label-side up every time (well, almost every time), if you secretly place a heavy coin in the bottom of the box between the drawer and the case. The weight of the coin causes the bottom of the box to fall downward.

Permit your barmate to toss first, and tell him you will pay for the drinks if you cannot match his toss. Naturally, you will win almost every toss.

THROUGH THE TUNNEL

Break open the cover of a match box and set it so that it forms a tunnel. Place the empty box drawer on the side of the cover opposite you.

Bet anyone to bring the drawer through the tunnel without touching it!

Here's how. Cup your hand in back of the drawer. Blow hard against the palm of your hand. The air will reflect and force the drawer through the tunnel.

TWO CENTS PLAIN

Balance two coins on the edge of a glass. Challenge someone to remove them both at the same time, using only the thumb and one finger of the same hand.

Grip the coins with the tips of the thumb and middle finger of one hand, causing them to slide down the side of the glass. Then draw them around the side of the glass and snap them together.

BOTTOMS UP

Lay a coin on the bottom of an inverted tumbler. Bet that it is impossible to lift the coin "from the top of the glass" with two matches.

Let them try it and lose. They did not lift the coin "from the *top* of the glass," but the bottom!

1000

Bet that you can write the number 1000 without lifting the pencil from the paper.

To do it, fold the edge of the paper down. Then trace the figure seen in Picture 1. When you lift the pencil, the number 1000 will appear on the bottom of the sheet.

THE ARCHITECT'S PUZZLE

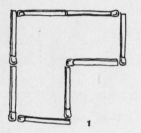
1

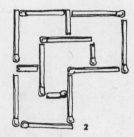
2

An architect's problem is to divide a lot equally. Let's help him! Arrange eight matches to form the figure in Picture 1. Hand your buddy four extra matches, and challenge him to *divide the area of the figure into four equal areas, each the same size and shape!*

His four matches may be broken in any way, but the original eight matches must not be moved.

See Picture 2 for the answer. Two of the matches are broken in half to do the job!

THE SECRET

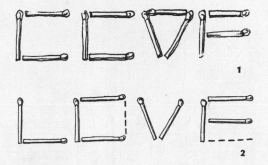

Using twelve matches, form Picture 1.

Now ask someone to rearrange the position of only two matches, and reveal the secret of *"what makes the world go round."*

The answer is "LOVE" (see picture 2)! LOVE is *really* the answer!

5 + 6 = 9

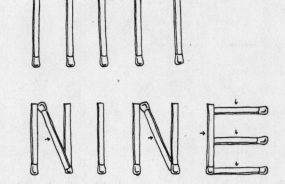

Challenge your friends to add 5 to 6 and make 9. Here's how. Lay five matches on the table, add the other six matches to spell out the word *NINE!*

THE SIX GLASSES

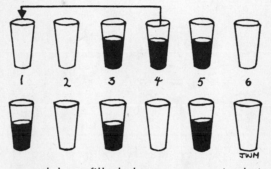

Three empty glasses and three filled glasses are required. Arrange the glasses from left to right: 1) empty, 2) empty, 3) full, 4) full, 5) full, 6) empty.

Now, challenge someone to arrange the glasses so they stand alternately one filled, one empty, one filled, one empty, one filled, one empty. *This must be done by touching or moving only one glass!*

Secret: Lift glass #4 and pour contents into glass #1. Replace #4 in its original spot.

THE FLYING MATCH

Place three matches as shown in the sketch, two of them thrust in between the drawer and the sides of the box. Light the cross match in the middle and bet which end will ignite first.

After all the opinions and bets are in, light the central match and watch the fun. The pressure of the other two matches will throw the burning stick in the air. The others do not light.

You win every time, since their bets never are correct.

BRIDGE OF KNIVES

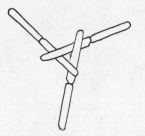 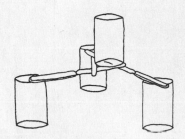

Using three glasses as bases, bet that you can form a three-way bridge, with three knives, each knife using a glass as its base.

The blades of the knives are interlocked, and the handles rest on the glasses.

KNOTS TO YOU

Bet someone that you can tie a knot in a handkerchief or a length of cord without letting go of the ends.

The secret: Fold your arms, grasp the ends of the handkerchief and unfold the arms without letting go of the ends. A knot will appear if done correctly.

SMOKE DREAM

Bet that you can cause a cigarette to smoke itself. Hold a lighted cigarette as shown, squeeze the palms together and relax them. Repeat again and again.

THE STRIPPER

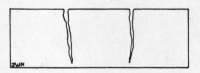

A three-inch strip of narrow paper is torn almost all of the way through in two places, each about an inch away from the other.

Bet anyone to completely tear the paper strip so that the center piece will fall free. You win every time!

No matter how they pull, the center piece will always stay fastened to one of the end pieces!

UNDER WATER

Here's a "swindle" which will keep them guessing until you tell the secret. Bet that *you can light a match under water!*

Have a glass of water held up high in the air, and merely light the match (under the water).

Now step back before the water is poured on your head!

TWO STRAIGHT ROWS

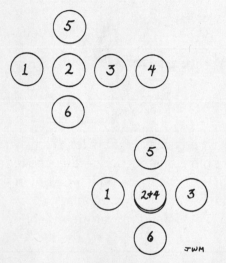

Arrange six coins, as in picture 1. Bet everyone that they cannot arrange the six coins, so that they form two straight rows of four coins each.

The secret is sort of a swindle. Place coin 4 on top of coin 2.

THE ACROBATIC FLAME

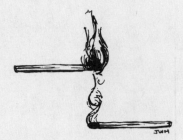

Bet your friends that you can make a match light by remote control.

Light two matches, blow one out and as the smoke rises hold the flame of the other match above it. The flame will slide down the curl of smoke and relight the lower match without direct contact.

Blow out the match again and repeat the relighting in "instant replay."

VANISHING SQUARES

Arrange twenty matchsticks to form seven squares (see picture 1). Bet that you can make two squares vanish, leaving only five squares, the same size as the original seven. *Only three matches may be moved!*

The way to do it is to remove three matches as in picture 2 and replace them as in picture 3.

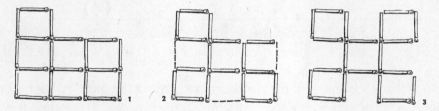

THE HOUDINI DIME

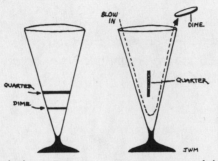

Set a dime in a tapered glass. Drop a quarter on top of the dime to entrap the dime within the glass.

Bet anyone to remove the dime without touching the quarter. Here's how: Blow down one side of the tumbler, causing the quarter to tilt over edgewise and the dime to slide out of the glass.

TOUCHDOWN

1) Can you place four golf balls so that each ball touches the other three?
2) Can you arrange five coins so that each coin touches the other four?
3) Can you arrange seven cigarettes so that each cigarette touches the other six?

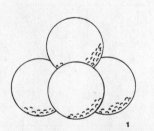

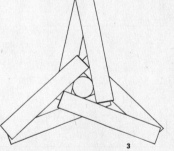

To win all three bets, place them as in the pictures.

THE MAGNETIC CIGAR

Bet that you can magnetize a cigar, and demonstrate by causing it to adhere to your fingertip.

Push a bent pin through the cigar band. The point of the pin rests on the fingertip. Throw away the pin and let them try it.

HENNY YOUNGMAN'S

BAR JOKES

If you must drink while you're driving home, be sure the radio in the car is turned up loud. That way you won't hear the crash.

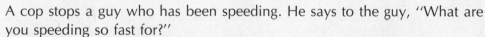

A cop stops a guy who has been speeding. He says to the guy, "What are you speeding so fast for?"

The guy says, "I'm sick."

The cop looks in the car and sees a racing form on the seat. "I see you have a racing form, and you're probably speeding to the track, and you say you're sick."

The guy says, "Oh, is that a sickness!"

There was a show in New York called "Oh Calcutta," where everybody on stage was naked. I wouldn't go to see that.

I went home, I looked in the mirror, I saved $50.00!

A hold-up man goes into the bank—he sticks a gun in the cashier's face, and says, "Give me all your cash."

The cashier says, "Here, take the books too, I'm $10,000 bucks short."

I discovered a new blood control device. My wife takes off her make-up.

A panhandler walks up to a man. He says, "Would you mind helping a man out of work? All I have in this whole world is this gun!"

BAR JOKES

A traveling salesman on the road stops off at a little restaurant. He orders two eggs.

They only have one egg left, so the waitress says to the chef, "Throw anything you have in the kitchen into it, he won't know the difference."

So the chef throws in a piece of old limburger cheese with the egg.

The man has his breakfast, and calls the waitress over. He says to the waitress, "Where do you get your eggs?"

She says, "We have our own chickens."

He says, "Do you have a rooster?"

She says, "No."

He says, "You better get one, because there's a skunk been fooling around with one of your chickens."

One fellow says to another, "Who was that lady I saw you with last night?"

"That was no lady, that was my brother-in-law. We're just sick about it!"

Linda Lovelace, star of "Deep Throat," says she's not going to make any more X-rated pictures.

She's had it up to here!

Elevator stops on the third floor and a nude woman walks into the elevator.

The guy in the elevator doesn't know what to say—he finally says, "My wife has an outfit just like yours."

A fellow goes to Confession—"Father, my wife and I took a vow we wouldn't have sex during Lent, and we broke our vow."

The Priest said, "What happened?"

"She was leaning over a potato sack, and she looked so cute, and as we're newlyweds, I couldn't help myself, and we made love there and then."

"What happened?"

"They threw us out of the A&P!"

BAR JOKES

A guy says to a Rabbi, "You have such a small congregation. How much do you make a week?"

The Rabbi says, "Six dollars a week."

He says, "How can you live on that?"

"If I wasn't a very religious man, and didn't fast three days a week, I'd starve to death!"

A mother says to her son, "Get out of bed and go to school."

He says, "I don't want to go to school."

She says, "Eight o'clock in the morning, you go to school."

"I don't want to go to school—the kids don't like me, the janitor don't like me, and the teachers don't like me."

"You're forty-five years old, and you're the principal. Go to school!"

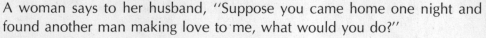

A woman says to her husband, "Suppose you came home one night and found another man making love to me, what would you do?"

He says, "I'd kick his seeing-eye dog!"

A man walks into his doctor's office and says, "Doctor, I have sex only once a week."

Doctor says, "How old are you?"

He says, "Seventy-three."

Doctor says, "You're seventy-three, and have sex once a week. I think that's wonderful. What are you complaining about?"

"My neighbor is seventy-six years old, and he says he has sex six times a week."

The doctor says, "You say the same thing!"

A young woman goes to a doctor.

The doctor says, "Get undressed."

She says, "Turn out the lights."

He says, "After all, I'm a doctor."

She says, "Turn out the lights."

So the doctor turns out the lights.

Five minutes later, she says, "Where shall I put my clothes?"

He says, "On top of mine!"

BAR JOKES

A guy has a dream that God told him to have himself fixed up. So the guy has a hair transplant, he gets a nose job, he reduces and becomes nice and slim, buys new clothes. All of a sudden, he is struck by lightning, and winds up in heaven.

He gets to heaven, and God doesn't even talk to him.

He shouts at God, "You told me in my dreams to better myself. I had a nose job, I had a hair transplant, I took off weight—now you don't even talk to me."

God says, "Don't holler at me, I didn't even recognize you, Irving."

In Kookamunga on top of a hill is the Kookamungan Guard.

On the other side is the Enemy Guard.

The Kookamungan Guard is shouting out, "Thirteen, thirteen, thirteen."

The annoyed Enemy Guard shouts out to him—"What are you hollering out thirteen all the time for? What does that mean?"

The Kookamungan Guard says, "Come over here, I'll show you." He says to the Enemy Guard, "Look over that cliff."

He kicks the enemy over the cliff. He starts hollering out, "Fourteen, fourteen, fourteen!"

A fellow from New York joins the army. He is in the army three days, and asks for a three-day leave of absence.

The Colonel says, "What are you, a nut from New York? You are in the army three days, you ask for a three-day pass?" To get a three-day pass, you have to do something sensational."

The next day, the guy comes back driving an enemy tank all by himself.

The amazed Colonel says, "How did you do it?"

He says, "I took one of our tanks and went towards the enemy. I saw one of their tanks coming towards me. The enemy soldier put up a white flag, I put up a white flag. I said to him, 'Do you want to get a three-day pass?' He says 'Yes,' so we exchanged tanks."

My wife wanted her face lifted. They couldn't do that, but for $800.00 they lowered her body.

A man goes to a psychiatrist—the psychiatrist says to the man, "What do you do for a living?"

He says, "I'm an auto mechanic."

The psychiatrist says, "Get under the couch."

The guy was talking to his friend, and said, "My wife is in the next room and is about to have a baby."

His friend said, "Where's the doctor?"

He said, "I don't need the doctor, I deliver the baby myself."

All of a sudden, a scream from the next room.

He rushes in. Five minutes later, he comes out, "It's a boy!" All of a sudden, another scream, he rushes in, comes out five minutes later, says, "It's twins this time." Another scream—he rushes in—he comes out, and says, "This time it's triplets!" Now, one more scream—he rushes out the front door.

His friend says, "Where are you going?"

"I want to find out how you shut the damn thing off."

A woman called another woman on the phone and asked her how she was feeling. The other woman said, "Terrible! My head's splitting and my back and legs are killing me and the house is a mess and the children are simply driving me crazy."

BAR JOKES

The caller said, "Lissen, go and lie down, I'll come right over and cook lunch for you and you get some rest. By the way, how's your husband, Sam?"

The woman said, "Sam? I got no husband, Sam."

The first woman said, "My goodness, I must have dialed the wrong number."

The complaining woman said, "Then you're not coming over?"

A 70-year-old man married a girl of 20, and immediately was given advice by his friends. One of them said, "If you want a happy marriage, you must take in a boarder." This appealed to the old man, and a few months later he met his friend who wanted to know how things were coming along.

The old man said, "Things couldn't be better, and I owe it all to your good advice."

His friend said, "I'm glad to hear it, and how's your wife?"

The old guy said, "Oh, she's pregnant."

His friend said, "That's great, and the boarder?" and the old man said, "Oh, she's pregnant, too!"

"I understand your husband got drowned and left you two million dollars. Can you imagine, two million dollars, and he couldn't even read or write."

She said, "Yeah . . . and he couldn't swim either."

A guy walks into the Stage Delicatessen, orders barley and bean soup. The waiter says, *Nemnisht,* which in Jewish means, *don't take it.*

The man walks over to the boss and says, "Where did you get the Chinese waiter who speaks Jewish?"

"Don't say anything, he thinks I'm teaching him English."

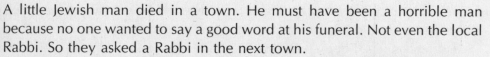

A little Jewish man died in a town. He must have been a horrible man because no one wanted to say a good word at his funeral. Not even the local Rabbi. So they asked a Rabbi in the next town.

He said, "I didn't like him either, but I'll say a few good words."

He gets up at the funeral and says, "His brother was worse!"

At our country club, one of the members dropped dead. Nobody wanted to tell his wife, so the doctor said he'd do it.

He called, and said, "Mrs. Cohen, your husband Sam lost $500 playing cards at the club."

The wife yelled, "He should drop dead."

The doctor said, "He did."

This Irish guy drops dead. Who should tell the wife—and how? A guy volunteers. He knocks on the door—a lady comes out—he says, "Is this the Widow Ryan?"

"I'm not the Widow Ryan."

"Wait until you see what they're dragging in the back door."

I knew a woman who went to an HMO, where they had about eight doctors. After 15 minutes in one doctor's office, she ran screaming down the hall. Another doctor, who finally got the story out of her, called the first doctor. "What's the idea of telling Miss Jones she's pregnant? She isn't. You frightened her to death."

"I know," the first doctor said, "but I cured her hiccups, didn't I?"

A salesman was trying to sell a bachelor a new car, and pointing to the dashboard, he said, "See this panel? All buttons! You press the red one and a redhead gets in the car with you. If you press the black button, a brunette gets in! If you press this yellow button, a beautiful blonde gets in the car."

The bachelor said, "Gee, that's great."

The salesman said, "Well, do you want the car?" and the bachelor said, "No, just sell me the buttons!"

Three scientists were given six months to live and they were told they could have anything they wanted. The first scientist was a Frenchman, and he wanted a beautiful villa on the Riviera, surrounded by gorgeous young girls. The second scientist was an Englishman, and he wanted to have tea with the Queen. The third was a Jewish scientist. He wanted the opinion of another doctor!

BAR JOKES

A movie producer advertised for a Texan, 6 feet tall, weighing 200 lbs. One morning, about 3 o'clock, he got a phone call in answer to the ad from a fellow who spoke with a Jewish accent.

The producer said, "You don't sound like a Texan," and the fellow said, "That's right, I ain't, I'm from New York."

The producer said, "Are you 6 feet tall and do you weigh 200 lbs.?" and the fellow said, "No, I'm five feet-five and I weigh 110 lbs."

The producer was furious as he yelled, "Then what the hell are you phoning me for, at 3 o'clock in the morning?" and the Jewish feller said, "I just called to tell you, ON ME YOU SHOULDN'T DEPEND!"

A traveling man went on the road for a month, but kept staying away. Every few weeks he'd send his wife a wire, saying, "Can't come home, still buying!" Every wire was the same, "Can't come home, still buying." This went on for three or four months, when his wife finally sent him a wire that said, "Better come home, I'm selling what you're buying!"

An elderly man approaches a prostitute. "How about a little fun?"
   She says, "How old are you?"
   He says, "Eighty."
   She says, "You've already had it."
   He says, "How much do I owe you?"

A minister gave a talk to the Lion's Club on sex. When he got home he couldn't tell his wife that he talked about sex, so he told her he spoke about yachting and boating.

   A few weeks later, she ran into some people in the village and they complimented her on the speech her husband made.

   She said, "Yes, I heard. I was surprised about the subject matter as he had only tried it twice. First time he got sick, and the second time his hat blew off."

BAR JOKES

A guy has a new pet, a little pussy cat, and he falls in love with the little pussy cat. The pussy cat follows him around, and he is just crazy about the pussy cat. The man wins a free trip to Paris and he leaves the pussy cat with his brother.

Two weeks later, he calls his brother from Paris. He says over the phone, "How is my little pussy cat?"

The brother says, "Your pussy cat died."

He says, "Why did you have to tell it to me that way for? You could have told me the pussy cat was on the roof, he broke his leg, and I would have gotten used to it, gradually."

The brother says, "Forgive me, I'm sorry."

"O.K., I forgive you. By the way, how is Mom?"

"She's on the roof."

A guy goes to court for a divorce. The Judge says, "Why do you want a divorce?"

He says, "Every night, when I come home from work, instead of my wife being alone, I find a different guy hiding in the closet."

The Judge says, "And this causes you a lot of unhappiness."

The man said, "It certainly does, Judge, I never have any room to hang up my clothes."

Girl fell overboard. Father said, "I'll give half my fortune to save her."

Fellow jumps in—saves girl.

"I'll keep my promise—here's half my fortune."

"I don't want money, all I want to know is who shoved me."

A rich old garment manufacturer died and his family met in the lawyer's office for the reading of his will.

He left $300,000 to his wife, $100,000 to his brothers, and $10,000 each to his sisters.

Then the will read: "And to my nephew Irving, who always wanted to be mentioned in my will, I say, 'Hello, Irving!' "

Sam got a dollar too much in his pay envelope and said nothing about it, but the following week the paymaster discovered his error, so he deducted a dollar from Sam's pay.

Sam put up a big squawk, so the paymaster said, "Funny you didn't complain last week when you were a dollar over," and Sam said, "That's right, because a guy can overlook one mistake but when it happens twice, it's time to complain!"

A guy asked another man, "What do you think of this Whitewater scandal?"

The other man, who stuttered, said, "They oughta oughta oughta take take take all all all those guys and throw throw throw them out of the government, and start start anew."

The other guy said, "That's easy for you to say."

A man goes down to a ship company. He wants to know the cheapest trip he can get to Bermuda.

The clerk says, "We can give you a suite for $2,500."

"No, that's too expensive."

"Well, we have a room for $500."

He says, "That's too expensive, what is the cheapest trip you have?"

"We have one trip where you get in a boat with 12 guys and you row across!"

A stockbroker catches his wife in bed with another man.

He says to her, "What's going on here."

"Believe it or not, John, I've gone public!"

A couple celebrating their fiftieth wedding anniversary—they go down to their old school—there, in a corner, was their old desk where he had carved on the desk, "I love you, Sadie," and he remembered where he had put her hair in the inkwell.

On the way home, a Federal Reserve truck's back door opens and money drops out. She picks up the money and counts it—$50,000.

The husband says, "Give the money back!"

She says, "No, finders keepers."

When they get home, she hides the money in the attic.

The next day, two FBI men show up at their home.

They say, "Pardon me, did any one in this house find any money that fell out of a Federal Reserve truck yesterday?"

She says, "No."

The husband says, "My wife's lying, she found the money and put it up in the attic."

She says, "Don't believe him, he's a little senile."

So they sit the man down and question him.

The FBI man says, "Tell us the story from the beginning."

The man says, "My wife and I were coming home from school."

The FBI man says, "Let's get the hell out of here!"

A dentist has been having a romance with one of his patients.

She is sitting in the dentist's chair, and he says, "Darling, we can't see each other any more, you're down to your last tooth."

BAR JOKES

A holdup man holds up a woman.
   She says, "I haven't got any money."
   He says, "I'll feel around your body, and see if you're telling the truth."
   Finally, he says, "Go ahead."
   She says, "Don't stop now, I'll write a check."

A man has been smoking cigarettes for 20 years. He takes one puff from a cigarette, throws it down and steps on it.
   He does this all day long. What do you think this man has today?
   Cancer of the shoe.

Two guys in a gym—one guy is putting a girdle on.
   His friend says, "Since when are you wearing a girdle?"
   "Since my wife found it in the glove compartment of my car."

A guy says to another guy, "How many times have you been married?"
He says, "Twice."
"What happened to your first wife?"
He says, "She fell in the wishing well."
I didn't know they worked!

A panhandler asks me for a dollar for a cup of coffee.
I start to follow him.
He said, "What are you following me for?"
"I want to be sure you don't buy a bowl of soup!"

Two furriers were returning from Miami, and just for the kick of it decided to take a taxi back to New York.
As they were climbing in the cab, one of them said, "Let me get in the cab first, I'm getting out at 72nd Street."

BAR JOKES

While playing golf today, I hit two good balls. I stepped on a rake!

Two fellows applying for a job as truck drivers.

One says, "This is my partner, Sam. My name is Orville."

"O.K., Orville, I want to give you a mental test. Suppose you are driving along a road at 3 o'clock in the morning, and you are on a little bridge, and another truck is coming towards you at 100 miles an hour, what is the first thing you'd do?"

"I'd wake up my partner, Sam, and say this is the greatest wreck you'll ever see."

Two soldiers are about to be shot by six enemy soldiers.

One soldier says to the other one, "I think I'm going to ask for a blind-fold."

The other says, "Sam, don't make trouble."

A man brags about his new hearing-aid. "It's the most expensive I've ever had—it cost $2,500."

His friend asks, "What kind is it?"

He says, "Half-past-four!"

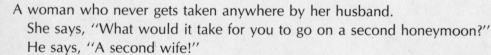

A woman who never gets taken anywhere by her husband.

She says, "What would it take for you to go on a second honeymoon?"

He says, "A second wife!"

BAR JOKES

Three women at a Hadassah dinner. One says, "My husband bought me an estate in Mt. Kisco, New York."

The other woman says, "I have a beautiful home up in Rye."

The third woman, who lives in the Bronx, says, "I live three stations from Scarsdale!"

A couple go to a doctor and complain that they are having trouble with their sex life, what can they do about it?

The doctor says, "The trouble with you people is that you don't communicate with each other. Make believe that you are making love on a yacht."

They get home that night, and as they are making love, he says to her, "Make believe we're out on a yacht out on the ocean." After a minute, he says to her, "Are you sailing yet?"

She says, "No."

A minute later, he says to her, "Are you sailing yet?"

She says, "No."

Another minute goes by, and he says, "Are you sailing yet?"

She says, "No."

He says, "Bon Voyage."

This guy dies and leaves the shortest will. It said, "Being in my sound mind, I spent my money!"

There is a man stretched out on his back on four seats in the theatre—the usher comes down, and says to him, "Mister, you will have to get out of those four seats; you are only entitled to one seat."

The man grunts, and doesn't move.

The manager of the theatre walks down. He says to the man who is still lying on the four seats, "Mister, you'll have to get out of there, all you're entitled to is one seat."

The man grunts, and doesn't move.

Now the policeman comes down. The policeman says, "Get out of those seats."

The man grunts.

The policeman says, "O.K. wise guy, where are you from?"

"The balcony!"

BAR JOKES

A little Jewish man gets on the bus—he sees a friend on the bus—he says to him, "You couldn't get a cab either!"

Two guys meet. One says, "You look bad, what's the matter with you?"

He says, "I was in London where there was a six-hour difference in time, and I couldn't sleep, and my timing is off. I sit down to eat, I get sleepy, I go to bed, I get hungry."

An airplane goes down and lands on the ocean ten miles from Germany.

The captain shouts over a microphone, "All those who can swim, get on top of the right wing. All those who can't swim, get on top of the left wing.

"You people who can swim, start swimming—you are only ten miles to shore.

"All those who can't swim—thank you for flying with us."

A man was taking a survey on the vaseline industry. He knocks on the lady's door. He says, "I represent a vaseline company and we are taking a survey of the many uses of vaseline in the home. Do you happen to use vaseline in your home, Madame?"

She says, "Yes."

He says, "How many ways do you use it?"

She says, "We use it for cuts, bruises and sex."

He says, "How do you use it for sex?"

She says, "We put it on the door-knob—it keeps the kids out of the room."

Vasectomy means never having to say you're sorry!

A fellow walked up to a tourist in New York and said, "Do you know where Central Park is?"

The tourist said, "No."

He said, "O.K., so I'll mug you here!"

A middle-aged lady goes to a doctor.

He says, "Get undressed . . . Lady, that's the ugliest body I've ever seen."

She says, "That's what my doctor told me."

"What did you come to me for?"

"I wanted another doctor's opinion!"

We've been married 45 years . . . went back to the same hotel where we got married . . . had the same suite of rooms . . . only this time *I* went in the bathroom and cried.

This prisoner is going to the electric chair.

The warden says, "You can have anything you want for your last meal."

The prisoner says, "I want strawberries."

The warden says, "Strawberries won't be in season for six months."

The prisoner says, "I'll wait."

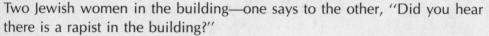

A man goes to the shrink and tells him that no one talks to him.
    The doctor says, "Next."

Two Jewish women in the building—one says to the other, "Did you hear there is a rapist in the building?"
    She says, "Yes I know, I already gave!"

Two guys at a bar, one says, "I don't know what's wrong with my wife, every time we make love she blacks out on me."
    His friend says, "Yeah, how about that?"

A guy owns a delicatessen. Two Internal Revenue men come to see him.
    The delicatessen guy says, "I slave all day to make a living for my wife and family, and you question my measly $6,000 a year income."

The tax guy says, "It's not your income we question, it's the six trips to Israel that you and your family made last year."

He says, "Oh that, I forgot to tell you we also deliver."

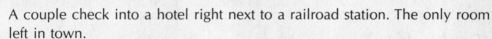

A couple check into a hotel right next to a railroad station. The only room left in town.

The man goes out to take a walk, the woman lies down to take a rest. All of a sudden, a train goes by at about 100 miles an hour and the vibration from the train knocks the woman out of bed.

Ten minutes, another train comes by so close that the vibrations knock her out of bed again.

She calls down and complains to the manager. She says, "What kind of a hotel is this? A train came by so close that the vibration of the train knocked me out of bed twice."

The manager sarcastically says, "I'd like to see that!"

She says, "Come on upstairs." He comes up. She says, "Lay down in that bed for a minute." He lays down.

Just then her husband walks in. "What are you doing in that bed?"

He says, "Believe it or not, I'm waiting for a train."

A Jewish woman had two chickens as pets. One chicken got sick, so she killed the other one to make chicken soup for the sick one.

Two drunks walking along Broadway in New York. One goes down into the subway by mistake. Comes up the other entrance and his friend is waiting for him.

The waiting drunk says, "Where were you?"

The other one says, "I was in some guy's basement. Has he got a set of trains!"

Want to drive somebody crazy? Send him a wire saying, "Ignore first wire."

In Hollywood they have community property. A couple gets divorced, she gets the Jaguar, he gets the little cap.

A drunk walked up to a parking meter and put in a dime. The dial went to 60. He said, "How about that. I lost 100 pounds."

A man and a woman in a room. All of a sudden, a knock on the door.

She says, "Quick, hide, that's my husband."

He says, "Where's the back door?"

She says, "We haven't got one."

He says, "Where would you like one?"

Two newlyweds—he's 64 and she's 23. She catches him cheating with a 48-year-old woman.

She says, "What has she got I haven't got?"

He says, "Patience!"

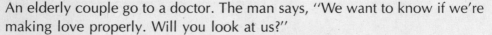

An elderly couple go to a doctor. The man says, "We want to know if we're making love properly. Will you look at us?"

The doctor says, "Go ahead." So they make love.

The doctor says, "You're making love perfectly. That will be $10.00."

They come back six weeks in a row, and do the same thing.

The seventh visit, the doctor said, "What are you coming here like this for —I told you you're making love properly."

The man says, "She can't come to my house, I can't go to her house. You charge us $10.00, the motel costs us $20.00, and we get $8.00 back from Medicare."

All you married men, want to drive your wives crazy? When you go home, don't talk in your sleep—just *grin*.

They have a new thing nowadays called Nicotine Anonymous. It's for people who want to stop smoking. When you feel a craving for a cigarette, you simply call up another member and he comes over and you get drunk together.

The two biggest features on the new cars are airbrakes and unbreakable windshields. You can speed up to one hundred miles an hour and stop on a dime. Then you press a special button and a putty knife scrapes you off the windshield.

A little old lady walked up to a cop and said, "I was attacked—I was attacked!"

He said, "When?"

She said, "Twenty years ago."

He said, "What are you telling me now for?"

She said, "I like to talk about it once in a while."

A woman called up the police department and said, "I have a sex maniac in my apartment. Pick him up in the morning."

Two drunks were standing in front of the Washington Monument. One of them started a fire at the base of it. The other said, "You'll never get it off the ground."

He said, "I love you terribly." She said, "You certainly do."

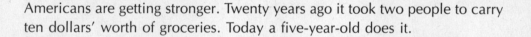

Americans are getting stronger. Twenty years ago it took two people to carry ten dollars' worth of groceries. Today a five-year-old does it.

In her own eyes, Peggy was the most popular girl in the world. "You know," she said, with characteristic modesty, "A lot of men are going to be miserable when I marry."

"Really?" said her date, stifling a yawn. "How many are you going to marry?"

A doctor gave a guy six months to live, and he didn't pay his bill. So the doctor gave him six more months to live.

A traveling salesman's car broke down on a lonely country road one night. It was storming but the salesman could see a farmhouse light not too far away. He made his way to the door and the farmer, being a friendly guy, invited the salesman in to have something to eat.

The farmer's beautiful young wife served a delicious meal and offered the salesman some homemade cottage cheese. The salesman having fully enjoyed the meal, replied that he would prefer putting it in the refrigerator for later.

The salesman asked the farmer if he could put him up for the night. The farmer apologized. The only place he had was in bed with him and his wife, but it was a large bed and there would be room if the salesman didn't mind. The salesman was delighted and graciously accepted.

As fate would have it, in the middle of the night the farmer had to get out of bed to tend a cow who chose that inopportune time to deliver her calf.

When the farmer had gone out to the barn, the farmer's lovely, alluring wife leaned over and whispered in the salesman's ear that now was his chance.

The salesman slyly smiled, and agreed. Whereupon, he jumped out of bed, raced to the kitchen, tore open the refrigerator, grabbed the cottage cheese, and ate it.

A doctor asked his woman patient, "Do you know what the most effective birth control pill is?"

She replied, "No."

He said, "That's it!"

An English flyer was shot down over Russia during the Second World War and wound up in a Russian hospital.

The doctor fixed him up but told him he would have to amputate his right leg to save his life.

After the flyer recovered from the shock of the bad news, he asked the doctor if he would do him one favor.

The doctor being a compassionate man said that he would try.

The flyer said, "Would you give the leg to one of your flyers and have him drop it over England. Hip, Hip."

The doctor agreed, and it was done.

A week later the doctor came in with the sad news that the other leg would have to be amputated also.

The flyer naturally was upset, but requested that the doctor please have one of the Russian flyers drop it over England with a Hip, Hip.

The doctor agreed, and it was done.

A month later the doctor came in again and told the flyer he was sorry but to save his life he would have to amputate his right hand.

The patriotic English flyer started to make his usual request, but the doctor interrupted him and said, "I'm very sorry but I can't grant your request this time."

The pilot asked, "Why not?"

The doctor replied, "They think you're trying to escape!"

Two friends meet on the street. One tells the other one, "Did you know Sam died?"

"Is that right. Did he leave anything?"

"Yeah, everything!"

HENNY YOUNGMAN'S

BAR TRICKS

HENNY'S PENNY

Here's a little stunt without preparation. A penny is caused to stick to the forehead as if it were glued there.

Simply press the coin to the forehead and move it upward.

P.S.: Dampening may help. Rub your fingers on the outside of your drink-filled glass to secretly obtain moisture.

THE MAGNETIC CIG

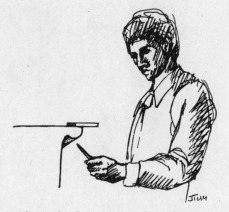

Set a cigarette on the edge of a bar. Secretly rub a pen on your coat sleeve. Now bet everyone that you can magnetize the cigarette. After the bets are in, hold the pen beneath the cigarette, and the cigarette topples from the bar top.

Now, try it with a pencil instead of the pen. Secretly blow on the cigarette while you hold the pencil beneath it.

The third time, secretly moisten the edge of the cigarette and let them try the stunt. Naturally, they can't!

GRAVITY DEFIED

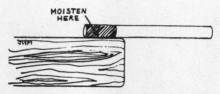

Moisten the edge of a cigarette, press it down on the edge of a table. It remains hanging over the edge in "outer space."

BETWEEN COURSES

Place a coin under a glass which is supported by two forks. Say that you can remove the coin without touching the glass or the forks.

Simply scratch the tablecloth in your direction. The coin moves slowly to you.

4 − 1 = 5

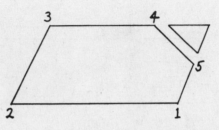

With a sheet of paper, you can prove that one from four equals five. Cut off *one* corner, and the paper now has *five* corners!

WOMAN'S LIB

First, a woman stands with her bent elbows locked tightly to her body. Two men, one on each side of her, can easily lift her off the floor by each grasping her elbow with one hand and her hand with the other hand.

Now comes the hard part . . . She can now resist the efforts of *five* strong men to lift her from the floor by allowing her arms to remain flexible and loose from the shoulders, and to relax the muscles.

THE TIPSY GLASS

MATCH
STICK

Can you balance a glass of liquid on edge? You can, if you secretly hide a match stick beneath the table cloth to aid it. A little practice is required, but well worth it!

WALLFLOWER

Have a young lady face the wall with her hands braced against the wall. With her body and arms held tightly in place, she can resist an entire row of men pushing against her back.

The ground rules are that they can only use one hand pushing against the person in front of them.

THE DENTIST'S DREAM

TAKE HOLD WITH TEETH HERE

With the glasses placed as seen, the bottom one filled with water, the question is to pour the water from B to A without handling the latter. Performance is accomplished by gripping A with the teeth and raising it to an upright position as shown and then pouring the liquid into it. Be careful of the added weight of the water, it may bring about disaster.

FIVE-FINGER LIFT

With our method, four men can lift a 140-pound woman using only five fingers.

One man stands behind her and places both of his index fingers under her arms. In a stooping position two men each place one finger under one of her feet. The fourth man lifts with one finger under her chin. *All lift simultaneously.*

TUMBLER

Practice this at home over a pillow. Push a glass tumbler off the edge of a table and cause it to fall on its rim. The shock will not break it if performed perfectly.

INERTIA

Stand an empty bottle upside-down on a handkerchief. Pull the handkerchief quickly. The bottle remains standing (sometimes)!

Here's another version of the same stunt:

PULL HERE

WONDERGIRL

A man stands in front of a woman and the man is challenged to lift the woman by the waist.

If she places her right hand upon the wrist of the lifter and the index finger of her left hand upon the jugular vein region in the neck and presses upon both points, the man cannot lift the woman, no matter how hard he tries.

THE BARTENDER'S LIFT

Here's the secret of lifting six beer glasses at once. Each of the fingers holds an outside glass while the inside pressure holds the center one.

STRONG BREATH

In this stunt, you propose to blow air through a glass of water. Set up a flaming candle with a glass of "aqua pura" in front of it. Blow at the glass and the flame extinguishes. Naturally, it is the air currents going around the glass, and not through it.

THE ATHLETE'S NIGHTMARE

Have a strong man double up his fists and place one over the other. A young boy or girl can separate the two fists every time, by simply snapping one finger of each hand against each of his fists simultaneously. The tighter he holds the fists together, the easier it is to separate them.

WHAT A WAY TO GET A DRINK!

A glass containing a drink of liquid refreshment is covered by another glass as shown. The problem is to remove the top glass and drink the contents without touching them with the hands.

The top glass is lifted with the chin and the bottom one is tipped on the edge of the table with the teeth so that you may imbibe.

HEADS UP

FLIP COIN UP

Remember George Raft's old flicks? Make a fist and place a coin on the back of the thumb. Now *toss* it—not spin it—into the air.

The coin falls in the *same* original position when it comes down to the waiting open fingers. The coin will wiggle and appear to spin.

HAND ON HEAD

It is practically impossible to lift a single hand placed firmly on top of the head. Try it with your favorite girl!

If both hands are clasped together with the fingers closely locked and held firmly down on the head, the entire body can be lifted by pushing upward under the arm at the wrists without the hands leaving the head at any time.

DON'T TOUCH ME

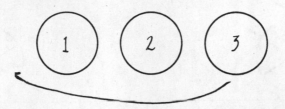

Place three coins in a row. Now challenge anyone to take away the middle one without touching it.

The answer is to remove the coin on the right (3) and move it to the left of the coin formerly on the left (1). You have therefore taken away the *middle* without touching it, because it is now the end, and the coin formerly on the left is now the middle coin. Get it?

ONE-LINER

 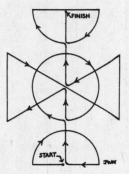

Try to draw the following design on the back of a napkin or menu with a single line, without lifting the pencil at all. Here's the design and the solution.

SNEAKY COIN SPIN

RUB FINGER

THUMB

This one is "sneaky." Balance a coin edgewise between the table top and the index finger. The coin will spin by rubbing the index finger with the index finger of the other hand.

However, it is really helped along by striking the coin secretly with your thumb during the rubbing motion.

UP AGAINST THE WALL!

Have all of your guests stand with both shoe heels square against the wall. Place a coin in front of each of them and then have them try to pick up the coin without removing their heels from the wall.

It's impossible, if they don't cheat!

HIGHWIRE ACT

This one requires a bit of practice. Balance a quarter between two needles (or toothpicks or wooden matchsticks), and cause the coin to spin by blowing on it.

THE EGG STUNT

Offer a dish of eggs to someone and ask him to spin one. It can't be done! Now secretly use a hardboiled one and it will spin!

CIG ASH GAG

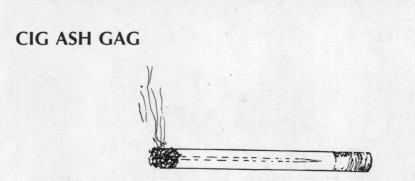

The test of a good *cigar* is the length of the ash that you get. Tell your friends to try to smoke a *cigarette* all the way down without dropping off the ash.

The secret is to insert a toothpick into the cigarette to hold the ash in place as it burns down!

MATCH MAGIC

Hold nineteen matches in your closed fist. Invite someone to select any number of matches between one and sixteen, while your back is turned away so you cannot see.

Now say "I have *as many as* you, and two more, and enough left over to make seventeen!"

No matter how many he chooses, you are always right!

KARATE CHOP

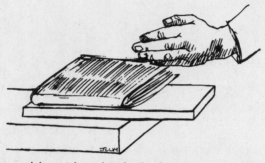

Lay a board upon a table with a third of it hanging over the side of the table. Lay a newspaper over the part of the board remaining on the table.

Tell someone to test their strength by hitting the board as hard as they can. It takes a very strong person to even move the board, let alone break it!

FINGERTIP JUGGLING

Place a two-inch square of stiff cardboard (or a playing card, if available) on your index finger tip. Balance a coin on top of the card, directly over the fingertip.

Snap the index finger of the other hand against the card edge. The card flies away, leaving the coin balanced on the finger! Cheers!

COIN-THROUGH-RING GAG

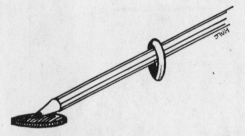

Challenge everyone to push a quarter through an ordinary finger ring.

Here's how . . . Stand the ring on edge. Lay the coin near the ring and shove a pencil through the ring. With the pencil, push the coin. You have *pushed the quarter through the ring!* Get it!

MAKE WAY FOR ME

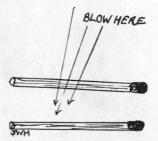

Two matches are laid on a table, about two inches apart. With your "secret power," you can pass your finger between them and cause the matches to move in opposite directions away from each other.

The secret is to blow lightly between the matches while you bend your head over them. The finger between the matches is just an excuse to cover the blowing "business."

THE BALANCING MATCH

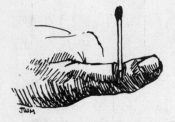

Place the small matchstick on the thumb and make stage play of great difficulty in keeping it balanced.

The thumb is bent down as shown in the sketch and the match is inserted in the wrinkle of flesh where it is firmly held in the upright position.

Then balance the match on the table surface. While the audience isn't looking, moisten the end of the match. When placing it on the table use some force in standing it upright. After the feat secretly remove the moisture with the finger.

THE PAPER BRIDGE

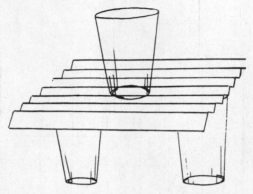

Arrange two drinking glasses about six inches apart. Place a sheet of paper over both glasses, forming a bridge. Challenge your guest to support a third glass on top of the "paper bridge."

After you have permitted everyone to try the stunt, corrugate it as shown and it will support the weight of the glass.

THE BALANCING CARD

With a toothpick or pin hidden between the ring finger and middle finger in an upright position, a card or matchbook can be balanced on the back of the hand. Challenge everyone to try it . . . but don't let them know about the secret.

ALL THE ANGLES

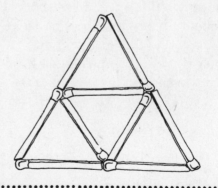

Ask your friends to form five triangles with nine matches. Give them the matches and let them try it. All the triangles are equilateral and none of the sticks must be broken. The solution of the puzzle is shown in the sketch.

A STICK "SHTICK"

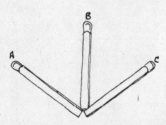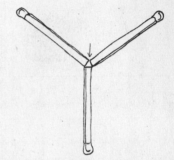

Place three matches in the sketch as shown and ask someone in the crowd to form an equilateral triangle with them by moving only the match marked "B." The other two must not be moved. Be sure that the ends are square.

Simply put match "B" at the bottom of the other two and a very small equilateral triangle will be formed by the square bases of the matches as shown in the sketch.

ONE-HANDED KNOT

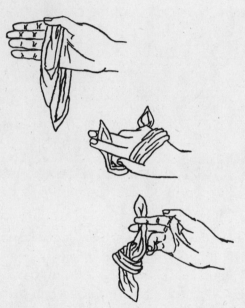

Challenge your cohorts to tie a knot in a handkerchief using only one hand.
To do it, just follow the pictures.

A STRETCHING STUNT

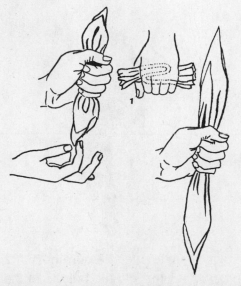

A handkerchief or dinner napkin is secretly folded in the hand as in figure 1. The handkerchief appears to stretch in size.

MATCH GAG

When you are lighting a cigarette offer the burning match to your friend who wants to share your light. He gets only the bottom of the match and you are left with the flame end!

   Ahead of time, break the match in half and begin the gag!

RAISE YOUR SPIRITS

Take an empty bottle and a paper straw (not bent or bruised). Challenge anyone to lift the bottle with the straw.

   The solution is to bend the straw about two inches from the end, and insert it, in the folded-over position, into the bottle. The extra section of straw wedges itself into the shoulder of the bottle. Lift the bottle using the straw as a handle. Applause!

MATCH THIS ONE

Challenge your buddies to balance a match book on its bottom end. The secret is to bend a match down in back of the closed packet.

Balance the booklet on the table or the palm of your hand with the bent match hidden from view!

ESCAPE ACT

Cut a hole the size of a dime in a sheet of paper. You then push a quarter through the dime size hole without tearing the paper!

BAR TRICKS

Here's the secret: Fold the paper in half at the hole area.

Simply bend the edges of the paper up and the hole will expand, and the quarter drops through.

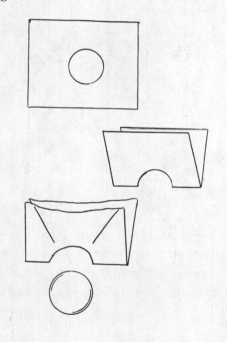

THE BALANCING GLASS

A little preparation is required, but you can have fun carrying this "trick" card with you in your wallet at all times.

Prepare the card at home by glueing a bent card to the back of another card. Balance the card on the table, and top it off with the glass.

THE MATCH HOUSE

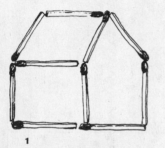

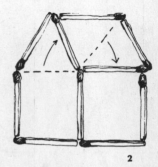

Take ten matches and form the little house in picture 1. The front of the house faces right. Let everyone try to make the house face *left* by changing the position of only two matches. The answer is seen in picture 2.

NINE PENNY PUZZLE

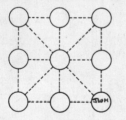

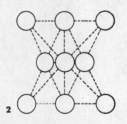

Arrange nine pennies in three rows of three coins each, forming eight rows of three (up, down and diagonally).

Challenge anyone to move just two pennies to form ten rows with three pennies in each row. The solution is shown in the sketch (picture 2).

THE TEEPEE

Split the ends of two matches and wedge them together. Then place a third one against them, forming the tripod as shown above. Ask someone to lift the three with one match. The solution is to let the loose match fall between the lifting stick and the two wedged ones.

To lift the three matches with their heads together, light them and extinguish the flame with a breath. The heads will be found to be welded together so that they may be easily lifted from the table.

KNIFE LIFT

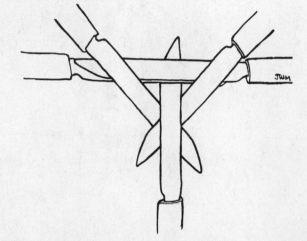

Challenge everyone to lift four table knives with one knife!
Weave the tips together as in the sketch.

TAKE A BREAK

Ask everyone to place a wooden match over the first joint of the second (middle) finger and under the first joint of the first (index) and third (ring) finger.

Then have them try to break the match this way. It's almost impossible!

About the Author

From the London Palladium to Las Vegas clubs, to Miami and Broadway vaudeville houses, over radio and television, and at more Bar Mitzvahs than he cares to recall, millions have rocked with laughter at Henny Youngman's jokes (and, in a pinch, at his fiddle!). "I started out in this business as a musician," he says, "but I was a lousy fiddler. People used to laugh at me. So I became a comedian."

Born in London and reared in Brooklyn, he entered show business at an early age and discovered that by not turning down any offers, he could work 300 days a year and get rich ("Frank Sinatra once told me that money isn't everything, and I said, 'Quite right, but you can't be rich without it' ").